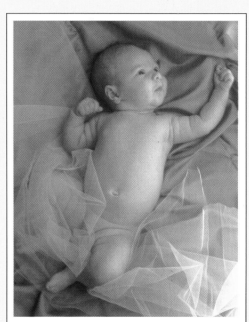

*Sleep, Little One*

ISBN 1-58987-073-5

Published in 2004 by Kindermusik International, Inc.

Do-Re-Me & You! is a trademark of Kindermusik International, Inc.

Printed in Mexico
First Printing, November 2004

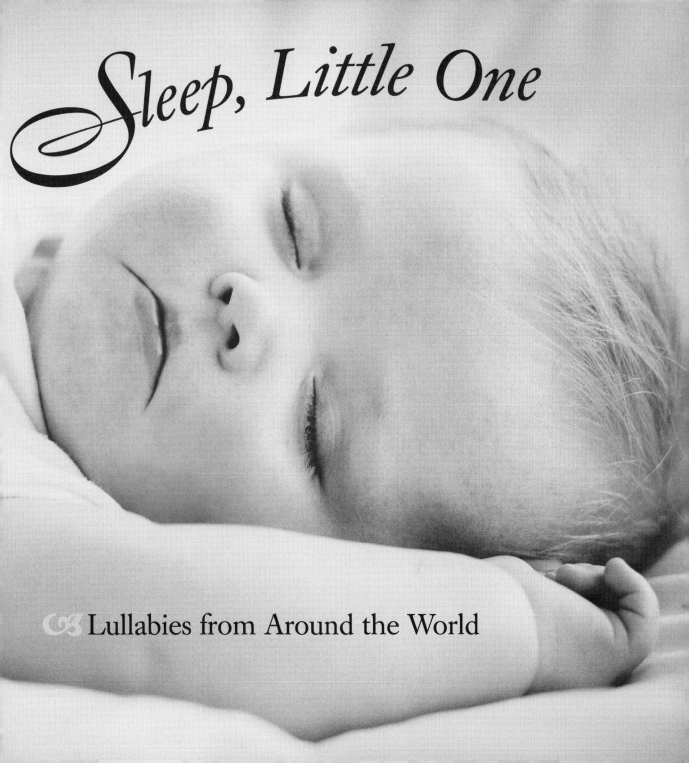

# Sleep, Little One

## ᏏᏯ Lullabies from Around the World

# O How Lovely Is the Evening

O how lovely is the evening, is the evening,
When the bells are sweetly ringing, sweetly ringing;
Ding, dong, ding, dong, ding, dong.

*Never fear spoiling children by making them too happy.*
*Happiness is the atmosphere in which all good affections grow.*
–Thomas Bray (1656–1730)
English clergyman and philanthropist

# Rurru

*Rurru que rurru que ruru ru rru.*
*Rurru que rurru que ruru ru rru.*

Lullaby, baby. O lullaby, dear.
Slumber, my baby. O slumber, my dear.

*Do you know what you are? You are a marvel. You are unique.*
*In all the years that have passed, there has never been another*
*child like you.*

–Pablo Casals (1876–1973)
Spanish cellist, composer, conductor

# Sleep, My Little One

Sleep, my little one, my loved one,
*Babuska Bai-O.*
As the bright moon watches o'er us,
*Babuska Bai-O.*

*Babuska Bai-O* is a Russian term of endearment.

*Is it not by love alone that we succeed in penetrating to the very essence of being?*

–Igor Stravinsky (1882–1971)
Russian composer

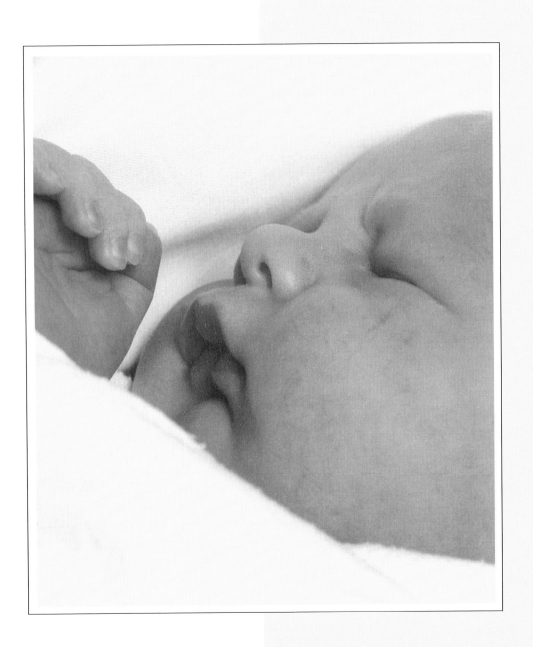

# Suliram

*Suliram, suliram, ram, ram,*
*Suliram yang manis,*
*Adu hai indung suhoorang*
*Bidjakla sana dipandang manis.*

Go to sleep, little one.
Close your eyes and dream tender dreams.
For you are protected by my love.

*I see the clouds, as white as cotton, floating in the big*
*wide sky. If I can reach up and grab them, I'll take*
*them home with me.*

–Indonesian song and nursery rhyme

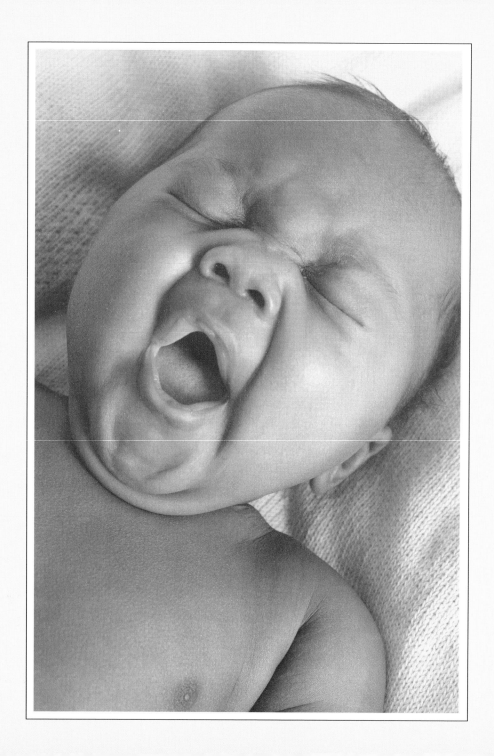

# All the Pretty Little Horses

Hushaby, don't you cry, go to sleepy, little baby.
When you wake, you shall have all the pretty little horses.
Blacks and bays, dapples and grays, coach and six-a-little horses.
Hushaby, don't you cry, go to sleepy, little baby.

*You rose into my life like a promised sunrise, brightening my days with the light in your eyes.*

–Mayo Angelou (1928–   )
American author and poet

# ais do-do

*Fais do-do, Colas, mon p'tit frère,*
*Fais do-do, t'auras du lo-lo.*
*Maman est en haut qui fait des gateaux,*
*Papa est en bas qui fait du chocolat.*

Go to sleep, Colas, my sweet little brother,
Go to sleep and you'll get a treat.
Oh, Mother's upstairs, some cookies she'll bake,
And Father's downstairs, sweet chocolate to make.

*Loving a child doesn't mean giving in to all his whims; to love him*
*is to bring out the best in him, to teach him to love what is difficul*

–Nadia Boulanger (1887–197
French musician and teach

# Que linda manita!

*Que linda manita que tiene el bebé,*
*Que linda, que mona, que bonita es.*

How pretty, how little, this sweet baby's hand.
So soft, oh so pretty, how lovely it is.

*Pequeños deditos rayitos de sol,*
*Que gire que gire como un girasol.*

Fingers so tiny like small rays of sun.
Around and around like a twinkling sunflower.

*I love you without knowing how, or when, or from where. I love you straightforwardly,*
*without complexities or pride; so I love you because I know no other way.*

–Pablo Neruda  (1904–1973)
Chilean poet

# Sleep, My Little Bird

Sleep, my little bird,
Close your drowsy eyes.
Eye loo, loo, loo.

Rest in peace, my child,
Under starry skies.
Eye loo, loo, loo.

I am always near,
So you need not fear.
Eye loo, loo, loo.

Sleep and have sweet dreams,
As the bright moon beams,
Full of light and love.
Eye loo, loo, loo.

*Every blade of grass has its angel that bends over*
*it whispering, "Grow, grow."*

–The Talmud

# Shining Moon

Shining moon, shining on the ground.
Baby, go to sleep now.
Mother, father, grandmother, and grandfather,
All will be busy working in the fields tomorrow.

You will be grown up very soon, little one,
And you will help your family care for the crops
And the cattle.

*If you plan for one year, plant rice. If you plan for ten years, plant trees.*
*If you plan for a hundred years, educate children.*

–Confucius (circa 551–479 BC)

Chinese philosopher

# Golden Slumbers

Golden slumbers kiss your eyes,
Smiles await you when you rise;
Sleep now, my little one, do not cry,
And I will sing a lullaby.

*Very young children have an artless beauty, an innocent grace,
an unstudied abandonment of movement.*

–Alan Alexander Milne (1882–1956)
British author

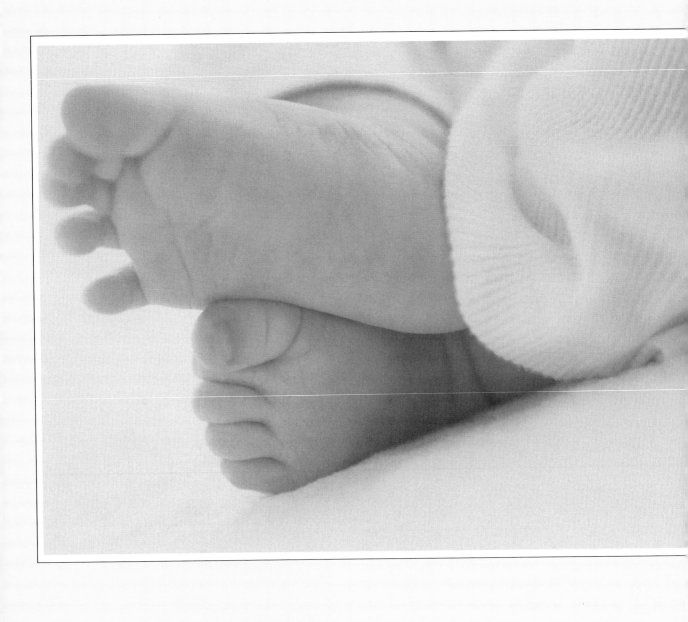

# Raisins and Almonds

To my little one's cradle in the night,
Comes a new little goat snowy white.
The goat will trot to the market
While mother her watch will keep,
To bring you back raisins and almonds.
Sleep, my little one, sleep.
To bring you back raisins and almonds.
Sleep, my little one, sleep.
Sleep, my little one, sleep.

*Show her the rudder, but don't steer her boat.*

–Yiddish proverb

# Latvian Lullaby

Lulla, lullaby, and dream, my little baby.
Lullaby and close your eyes and dream, my little baby.

*All year round I gathered songs,*
*Waiting for Midsummer Night.*
*Midsummer Night is here at last.*
*It's time to sing all the songs.*

—excerpt from a Latvian folk son

# *Ally Bally*

Ally bally, ally bally bee,
Sittin' on your daddy's knee.
Greetin' for a wee penny,
To buy some Coulter's candy.

*When the first baby laughed for the first time, the laugh
broke into a thousand pieces and they all went skipping
about, and that was the beginning of fairies.*

–James M. Barrie (1860–1937)
Scottish dramatist and novelist

#  Duérmete, mi niño

*Duérmete, mi niño,*
*Duérmete solito,*
*Que cuando despiertes te daré atolito.*

Go to sleep, my child,
Sleep in peace and dream.
For when you awaken,
I will give you cream.

*One does not love one's children just because they are*
*one's children, but because of the friendship formed while*
*raising them.*

–Gabriel Garcia Marquez (1928–   )
Columbian novelist

# May There Always Be Sunshine

May there always be sunshine.
May there always be blue skies.
May there always be Mama.
May there always be me.

*The soul is healed by being with children.*
–Fyodor Dostoevsky (1821–1881)
Russian novelist